INSTEAD

By Dennis Blount

ISBN-13:
978-1979712668

ISBN-10:
1979712662

DISCLAIMER

This book is designed to provide hope to its readers. It is a true and personal account of the lives of Dennis, Layna and Hailey Blount.

DEDICATION

I dedicate this book to my daughters; the two that kept me
going in the right direction in the most difficult times of my life.
Thank you Layna and Hailey Blount for standing by me through
thick and thin.

Thank you both for your unconditional love and support.

Love you both forever.

Dad

FORWARD

I remember the day we went to the hospital expecting to hear the joyous news that we were getting another great niece. Instead of getting good news, we were told that the baby might not live. She was born with a condition that we had never heard of. We did not know what a diaphragmatic hernia was. Whatever it was, she had only a slim chance to survive. Thanks to the saving grace of our Lord and Savior Jesus Christ and the marvel of medical science that problem was solved.

When she finally was released from the hospital, she came home with a feeding tube attached directly to her stomach because she was unable to swallow. When her Mom wanted to go somewhere that she could not take the baby (because of all the medical paraphernalia) she had to get a babysitter. She could not get just anyone; she had to get someone who could manage all the equipment. Evelyn and I were privileged to be among the ones who could care for her. Her Mom did not want people who would be amused by the baby's condition to keep her.

As she grew older we learned that she had another problem we had never heard of, Mitochondria.

This was a problem that medical science could not solve. When a child is born with as many strikes against it as Layna had, we are sure to ask, 'What will become of this child?' We can see that Layna has turned out well in spite of her beginning. The pages of this book will inform us of the obstacles she had to overcome and how well she has overcome them. As she grew up she was drawn to horses. But how could such a small girl easily handle large horses? We are amazed at how well she is able to race them and how often she wins races.

The author of this book is her Daddy (my nephew) and he knows her well. He has worked beside her and helped her when necessary. Instead of discouraging her when she wanted to try difficult things, he has encouraged her and helped her achieve things that people with her disabilities could not possibly do.

As you read this book, you will be inspired and encouraged if you have similar obstacles to overcome. There is no limit to what you can achieve if you put your faith in God and never give up.

Roland Blount (Uncle to Dennis Blount)
Retired Missionary

INTRODUCTION

I don't look at myself as an author and poet. I'm blessed to be the instrument and vessel that God has chosen to write these words. I'm a country boy cowboy raised on a little farm in Durant, Florida inspired by the God of Abraham, Isaac, and Jacob to write for His glory.

In this book you will find a child of God facing death at her birth. 18 years later she faces death once again. You will read about Gods miracles of healing. I'm amazed everyday watching her live her dream. She fights and wins everyday with the help of her Savior Jesus Christ. Her determination to live and go forward is beyond measure.

I would like to thank and express much appreciation to all of the doctors, nurses and hospital staff that God used to work His miracles through for Layna. Arnold Palmer's Children's Hospital Orlando, FL, Tampa General Hospital, Tampa FL, Scottish Rite Children's Hospital, Atlanta GA. Layna would not be here today if it were not for these great health care facilities and their professional staff.

I would also like to give thanks and appreciation to the sponsors that have helped Layna thus far. Bills Prescription, Brandon, FL, Jeff Riley Irrigation, Plant City, FL, Brandon Water Systems, Plant City, FL, Brandon Air, Plant City, FL and Brenda Simmons, Plant City, FL. Layna has accomplished much more because of their generosity and compassion.

Raised in the Country
A Poem by Dennis Blount

I was born and raised in the country
where the creeks flow to the river.
Where the cows, horses and wild game roam.
Where mother earth is the life giver.
I wouldn't trade it for the city with all its

shimmering lights and gold.

I've got the sun, moon and stars.

What a beautiful sight to behold.
Where babies grow up to be farmers and ranchers.
My playground, I call stomping ground.
Miles and miles, I can roam.
A place where God's creation is found,

born and raised in the sticks.
With a tree house down below county boy to the bone,
winding trails I would go.
Ball games in the pasture.
Country boys and girls from all around,
trees and bull holes for bases,
where the cow patty is found.

Cane poles, wigglers and bream
wading up and down that creek
but when the sun goes down
to my girlfriend's house I would sneak.

Good life in the country, can you smell that bacon fry?
Sitting around a camp fire somethings money just
can't buy.

Heading out down to the creek,
swimming holes up and down,
canoeing down the river where the rope swing is found.

It's a blessing to be raised in the country.

Roots of the family tree,
only country fold would understand.
I thank God, he chose me with
freedom, red, white and blue
and all the country folk like me
that were born and raised in the country
I'm sure would all agree.

Layna's passion and love for horses started in her family far back as I know with her great-great-grandfather, M.L. Blount. A pioneer, innovator, mountain man, and cowboy he was. I was told that he also was a born again believer and that he founded and brought Pentecost from Wimauma Church of God to what is now Pleasant Grove Assembly of God, my home church.

My Great Granddaddy M.L. Blount and Great Grandmother Nancy Jane, Aunt Eva and Granddaddy Clearance Blount

It's my understanding that he and his brother rode horses from South Carolina down to Tampa, Florida in search of a homestead back in the late 1800's. From me hunting off horseback I could ride about 20 miles in eight hours. On the 3rd day my bottom side became so sore I had to ride the stirrups most of that day. From my calculation it must of took them about a month of hard riding to make it down to Tampa. Cowboys have to be tough to endure such rides. M.L. Blount settled on a 160-acre homestead in Durant, Florida. His son, my uncle Lovic Blount, told me the story.

Kelly Falkner was the bell ringer at Pleasant Grove Camp Meeting 1928

*On the left is my Granddaddy Clearance Blount
and his brother Uncle Loui on the right*

*My only win picture age 15 years old. Turned 16 and gained 40 lbs. over night.
My Jockey career was over.*

1970 Calumet Farm - It was a pleasure to meet this Triple Crown Winner!
Me, Benda and Denise

1970 Claiborne Farm, Paris, KT - Daddy, Mama, Denise, Brenda and Me
with horse 'Buck Passer'

He also told me that his dad broke, trained, bought, sold and bred horses to pay for the homestead and to make a living. He said that him and my grandfather, Clarence Blount, and sister took care of most of the crop farming and milking cows. He must have had a great love and passion for horses to make a living with them. His children and grandchildren didn't have much interest in horses except for my dad, C.E. Blount. My dad has lived on part of the homestead his entire life. Layna and I have also lived on part of the homestead our entire lives. A heritage we are all proud of. Part of the land we live on my granddaddy Clearance Blount bought from Cumberland Lumber company. That land joined the homestead land that my great granddaddy M.L. Blount took over. Regardless of how much of the homestead land we live on, it all happened on Blount Rd.

Pleasant Grove Camp Pole Barn Church

2017 Pleasant Grove Church

It was told to me that around 1900 my great granddaddy went south to visit the Wimauma Church of God Camp Meeting. While he was their he received the Baptism in the Holy Spirit with evidence of unknown tongues of fire. When he offered it to his pastor and congregation at the Methodist church he attended they wanted nothing to do with it. M. L. Blount being the innovator he was went across Turkey Creek Rd. in Plant City (with half the congregation following him) and built a pole barn. It was then and there that Pleasant Grove Camp was born. God blessed the grounds and His anointing still lives there today at my church, Pleasant Grove Assembly of God.

I must say more about what the Lord has done for my family. I was 15 years old at the time. Close to my 16th birthday

INSTEAD   - 9 -

and getting a car. Only the Lord knew what I was going to do next. That was to fall in a world of sin head over heels, and boy did I.
What God had done before I made the fall was amazing. One Sunday after a service at Pleasant Grove Assembly of God I found myself at the altar. It was an unusual day because typically after service the alter times were loud. This altar service was particularity quiet. Unusually quiet. On a normal Sunday Pastor Wallace, Sister Mame Williams and others would be loudly (like Pentecostals are) working the altars blessing those searching for the Lord or just wanting more of the Lord. As I was quietly praying for the Lord's guidance I suddenly spring straight up and started speaking in unknown tongues of fire. I was freaking out because I knew 300 present eyes were all on me. I said Lord what's going on? **He said to me, "I'm real, I'm alive, I'm going to use you one day and don't you ever forget it".**

Believe me there hasn't been a day gone by in 45 years that I haven't thought about what He said. Never really or totally understood what he meant. I'm thinking now I'm just starting to understand. Through the years I have learned more about tongues of fire. Like prayer language and messages and interpretations during a service. It really brings a good impact to a service. It just makes a good service better when God shows up like that. I'm thankful for my great granddaddy and his boldness to keep and spread that same fire that I have. To this day, God's Will has been done and is still being done at Pleasant Grove Assembly of God. His Word there has been kept Holy.

My dad said as he grew up it was his responsibility to trim using a hammer and chisel and groom the horses and mules that were used for farming crops. His dad would let his children trail ride the horses and mules on Sunday afternoons. He told them not to run them. My dad had a passion for horse racing and didn't always do what he was told. He said his mama whipped him every day for something he would do wrong. Knowing this helped me understand why I stayed in trouble growing up. Believe me I got my share of whippings also.

There was a bush track for horse racing just a mile or so through the woods from where they lived. The horse races were scheduled on Sunday afternoon. His dad and mom being Christians would not allow my dad to go to the races on Sunday. My dad said that sometimes on Sundays him and his cousin, Malcom Porter, would sneak through the woods and sit in trees close to the track and watch the races.

When I was born my dad sold a horse to pay the hospital bill. I've been surrounded by horses ever since.

Love of a Mother
A Poem by Dennis Blount

God made man
to lead his family, the right way
Then he made a Mother
all in the same day

He thought Mother's were very special
they cook, mop and clean
There is a lot of little things they do
which stay unseen

After Dad goes to work
that's when her day begins
Changing diapers and feeding babies
talking on the phone to friends

Then lunch time comes around
the dinner bell rings
Mothers are busy in the kitchen
busy all the time it seems
After a long hard day
the school bus stops by
the kids come running in
shes so tired she could cry

But once again
day after day
It's the love of a Mother

and its here to stay

She says how can I help you?
are you hungry inside?
I have peas and corn
and chicken fried

Their love is beyond measure
it covers a multitude of wrong
After her tender love and care
all the pain is gone

So thank all the Mothers
all across this land
Because without Mothers
homes would never stand.

HAPPY FATHER'S DAY

WHEN I WAS JUST A LITTLE BOY
MY DADDY USE TO PLAY WITH ME
HE WOULD TOSS ME UP IN THE AIR
I WAS HAPPY AS I COULD BE

HE TAUGHT ME HOW TO RIDE A BIKE
HE TAUGHT ME HOW TO RIDE A HORSE
HE TAUGHT ME HOW TO CATCH A FISH
AND HOW TO MOW THE YARD OF COURSE

MY DADDY WAS THE BEST PROVIDER
THE FOOD WAS ALWAYS THERE
HE ALWAYS HAD THE ANSWER
HE ALWAYS SEEMED TO CARE

HE GAVE ME GOOD ADVICE
I WAS NEVER LED ASTRAY
ALWAYS WORDS OF WISDOM
AND HE'S JUST THE SAME TODAY

MY CHILDREN CALL HIM PAPA
THEY LOVE HIM WITH ALL THEIR HEART
THEY ALWAYS ASK A LOT
AND HE ALWAYS DOES HIS PART

I'M PROUD TO CALL HIM MY DADDY
I'M ALWAYS GLAD TO SAY
I LOVE YOU WITH ALL MY HEART
AND HAVE A WONDERFUL FATHER'S DAY

Dennis Blount

Thank you Mama
A Poem by Dennis Blount

A sweet lady went to Tampa
Back in November 1957
Laying in a hospital bed
Waiting for a miracle from Heaven

She said I will go through the pain
And pay whatever the cost

Trusting in my Lord Jesus
Trusting the cross

Then her son was born
As the tear drops fell
A true moment of love
On her face, you could tell

So she took him in her arms
And held him close and tight
Thanking her Lord Jesus
Oh, what a precious sight

So then she took him home
A place where he could live
The Lord said put him in My hands
For her, he was hard to give

As time went on
He grew strong and bold
Finally, one day she looked
Her son was too big to hold

So then she cried out to Heaven
My son has gone astray
I plead the blood of Jesus
Each and every day

Trusting the Lord
Praying everyday
Looking for a miracle
A warrior you could say

Sin took its toll
But Mary stood her ground
With the faith of Abraham
Her son was finally found

She wraps her arms around him
Thinking, it was worth it all
The time she spent on her knees
God finally answers her call

Thank you Mama for all your prayers
God says everything's okay

I'm going to say I love you
And wish you a Happy Mother's Day.

To Me She Was Mama
A Poem by Dennis Blount

In an unknown tongue,
I could hear her voice
I walked by her bedroom window
as she made the choice.

To be a Prayer Warrior day in and day out
Crying out to the Master,
you and I, it was all about

For hours and hours
Every single day
She would be on her knees
Giving her life to pray

I was just a little boy
Didn't quite understand

But as I know now
It was all in God's plan

She never criticized anyone
Speaking words of love
Full of God's wisdom

Like a heaven-sent dove
Who's going to fill her shoes?

Who's going to pay the cost?
Who's going to give their time
praying for the lost?

She's gone but not forgotten!
Remembering her will surely live on
That strong faithful woman,
my blood, flesh and bone

Heaven is rejoicing as she passes on through
Glorious gates of Heaven
With a heart that's true

Mary Elizabeth Blount,
she certainly won her race
To me, she was Mama
Thank God for His Mercy and Grace!

Good times I remember growing up was when my dad, my mom Mary, and two sisters, Denise and Brenda, and I would go trail riding with cousins and friends on weekends. I was about 12 years old when my dad paid $50 for his first grade race horse. Mr. Trouble was his name and he could fly. He would flip back out of the starting gate so my dad ran him with a flipping halter. One time the flipping rope broke. My dad grabbed me by my arm and pulled me to safety as Mr. Trouble flipped on out to the ground. I believe my dad saved my life that day. That ended Mr. Trouble's racing career.

Mr. Trouble – me riding him and my sister Denise and cousin Pam Porter Varvel on my mom's horse Missy at Plant City Strawberry Festival Parade

My Mom's horse Missy with cousins James, Dorinda and my sister Brenda

Last quarter horse racing event at Pompano Park, Pompano Beach FLA. Was in 1991. My dad ends up receiving awards for being number one trainer of the meet and owner and trainer of the horse of the meet Oh Jays Magic who set the track record at 300 yards. I was super proud of my dad for his accomplishments with racing quarter horses. Anytime I have a question about horses I ask my dad and if I have one about barrel racing, I ask Brenda Simmons.

My Dad Gene Blount with one of his race horses

They seem to always have the answer. I've been blessed to be surrounded with good equine knowledge my entire life.

My mother Mary Blount and Layna

My mother Mary Blount R.I.P. passed on to glory April 29, 2016. As you all know it is an extremely hard time in life. She will always be missed. At times she would cowgirl up and trail ride with the family. Never forget the time my dad, mom and I were on a trail ride not far from our farm. I made the wrong decision and decided to switch my mom's horse missy from behind. She kicked up striking me in the knee, knocking me off my horse. At age 14 I learned quick to respect even the gentlest horses. Waddled 3 months with crutches, saddest past was, it was the last day of school starting 3 months of summer vacation. I could not believe I was stuck in the house all summer long.

One day as a group of us were trail riding going down the trail of a 40-foot pit bank Mr. Trouble decided to jump off the bank and flipped upside down and we both rolled to the bottom of the bank. After my dad saw we were ok, he said, "you couldn't find an easier way to come down?" He was full of it. As I got back on everyone shook their head and laughed and we rode on.

Another funny time was when my dad was on big John and was going to teach him to shoot off of and deer hunt with him. In our pasture a rabbit jumps up running. My dad shot at the rabbit and big John took off running. It was funny to watch my dad roll off the back and hit the ground. I could go on and on with funny stories like this.

Layna at 2007 Youth World with Hailey climbing the fence in the background

Dennis, Hailey and Layna Blount

Diamond in the Rough
A Poem by Dennis Blount

She's a diamond in the rough

Special in many ways
She's a sister to a miracle

She defends her with no delays
Dysfunctional family
Hard road to walk
But she has persevered
Battle well fought
She leans on the lord
On her knees she prays
Asking God for direction

In his hands she stays
A dad so blessed to have such a queen
Her name is Hailey
A daddy's dream

She's a country girl too

Got a heart of gold
Give the shirt off her back
God threw away the mold
She's a barn yard girl

Can ride a horse real fast
Flipped my golf cart one time
Funny things of the past
Life is not always fair
Bad times come and go
But she's my little queen

And I love her so
She's a diamond in the rough

Speaks loud and bold
Daddy's little queen and my pleasure to hold

As time went on I got married to my 3rd wife April. Together, we have two children, my only children, Layna and Hailey. April and I are divorced but get along well enough and we both do our best to make a good life for our daughters.

Layna was born 1992 with a diaphragmatic hernia with a five percent chance of living. When she came out she didn't cry but we sure did knowing something was wrong when they rushed her out of the room. Come to find out Layna had a hole in her diaphragm. Her stomach with intestines where all in her chest. Her lungs could not grow and develop causing her to have only about a ¼ of a lung. She could not breathe. We all turned to our Heavenly Father pleading for grace and a miracle.

From Brandon Hospital they rushed her to Arnold Palmer Children Hospital in Orlando, Florida. We were blessed that they had an extracorporeal membrane oxygenation (ECMO) machine available there. ECMO takes 80 percent of the work off the heart and lungs while pumping blood and oxygen through the body. The tubes were hooked to an artery in her neck. As her lungs grew they weaned her off the machine. Staying with cousins in Orlando, April and I were back and forth to the hospital each day.

Back then one in a million babies were born with a diaphragmatic hernia. It's like one in ten thousand these days.

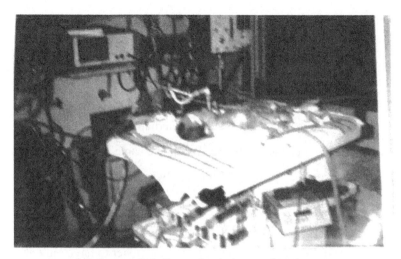

Baby Layna at birth. Her precious body covered in tubes.

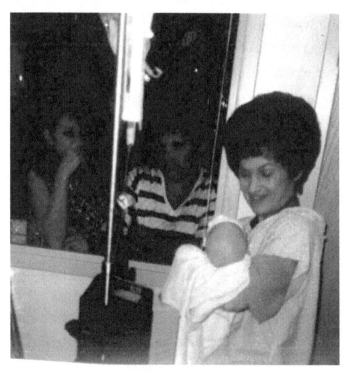

My mother Mary (Layna's Granny) loving on Baby Layna

Brandon Hospital – April holding Layna
Great Granddaddy Ray Ford Noble, Great Grandmother Beulah Noble and April's
Dad Layne Noble

Baby Layna

Many, many prayers were steadily going up for Layna.
Prayer requests were sent over to Carman in concert in
Orlando at the time. You know my mother, Mary Blount, was
all over Layna with some
prayer. My mother gave
testimony saying there was
an older nurse there
working at the time. The
nurse told her she could see
that we believed in God and
miracles. In other words,
when my Mama prayed
demons would tremble for
miles around. Sometimes I
would. She knew how to

get ahold of God. The nurse went on to say that she had never been to church or read the Bible. She said she didn't know anything about God or miracles. She said I've been a nurse most all my life and have seen a lot of drain tubes. The drain tubes coming out of your granddaughter's chest are supposed to drain blood and fluids off the surgery that was done to put Layna's stomach parts back in place. She said it's all been clear fluid not one drop of blood. She said, "if there is any such a thing as a miracle, that's got to be one". **Praise the Lord.**

With God in control Layna has been used as a witness since the day she was born. About two weeks had gone by and we were getting run down and weary. I said to April maybe we could go home for a night and come back tomorrow evening. The love of a mother came out and she said, 'no way am I leaving my baby but you can go'. I left because I just needed to go to the barn for a little while and gather my thoughts.

God truly knows our limits because the doctor came to us that same day saying they had Layna weaned down to 20 percent machine and if she sustained through the night they would take the machine off in the morning.

Understand, they had five diaphragmatic hernia babies enter the hospital there and when the machine was taken off all five of those babies bled to death in five minutes. It was a critical time. Layna needed a miracle. The doctor said if we can stop the bleeding in time Layna could live.

Faith in God rose up in me and I remembered what my mama had taught me. I said, 'what if my baby doesn't bleed'? The doctor said, 'that will have to come from a Higher Power'. I said, 'it's on the way'. My baby will not bleed in Jesus name. Prayers made it to the Throne Room of God because, Praise the Lord, she didn't bleed a drop.

The doctor told us Layna would have to come back in five to six years because as she grew the Teflon patch would tear loose from her diaphragm and they would have to put in a larger patch. With all my faith, I said, 'no she won't be back, in Jesus name. She will be Gods complete miracle'. Praise the Lord she never had to go back.

As God was working in the miracle they moved Layna the next day back to Brandon Hospital so while under observation she could be close to her family. Her mother spending practically all day with her baby was very happy about that. The whole time Layna was fed her mother's breast milk that had been pumped off through a feeding tube. The breast milk was pumped directly into Layna's stomach.

Layna finally came home but still with a pump and feeding tube. She was about six months old when she started eating baby food.

FOR WITH
GOD
ALL THINGS
ARE
POSSIBLE

MARK 10:9?

April holding Layna asleep on her horse

Me and Layna, asleep on her horse

Her daddy being a cowboy, it wasn't long before I had her in the saddle and she loved it. I know Layna was born with the passion for horses. Her first word was horse. As Layna grew up she spent a lot a time at the barn with her papa and his race horses.

Hailey and Layna

Layna walking their horse with Hailey riding

For several years, we had My New Car standing stud at our farm. I went to his stall one day. My dad was cleaning the stall and Layna was climbing up My New Cars front leg while he was eating. He didn't seem to mind but I liked to have had a heart attack. I ask my dad if she was okay? He said, 'sure - she does it all the time!' Trusting my dad, I was okay with it.

*Layna on **This Cars Trouble***

Soon after that incident there was another. My dad was
leading This Cars Trouble with Layna up. He was a level headed,
easy going colt. They were going around the galloping ring when a
neighbor nearby started throwing a box down and caused the colt
to jump out from underneath Layna and she hit the ground. It was
a pretty high fall for a little girl four to five years old. She jumped
up crying and ran to the house where her granny was. Her papa
was hollering for her to come back and get back on. (Our walk in
life can be the same way. We all fall short sometimes. We just
have to get up and get back on with our life even though
sometimes it hurts. Because life goes on.) About ten minutes goes
by. Sure enough here she comes. She said papa put me back on.
Her papa said that's what cowgirls do. It takes nerves of steal to
cowgirl up. That day Layna walked through her fears at a very
young age. When her love and passion for being a cowgirl kicked

in, she got it done. After that day she was ready to get on just about anything.

Another time was I would sit her in the saddle with me and took her on about a four-mile trail rides. She would fall asleep on my shoulder after about two miles down the trail. In the saddle she was right at home.

In 1997 Hailey was born. Sure enough it wasn't long before I had Hailey in the saddle. At about three years old she loved riding with me while gathering cattle. At Turkey Creek Stable team pinning, we would gather cattle at the start of each run and race back to the gate. She loved it.

My Dad and Mom (Gene and Mary Blount)
Layna and Hailey, Reese, Denise and Mason

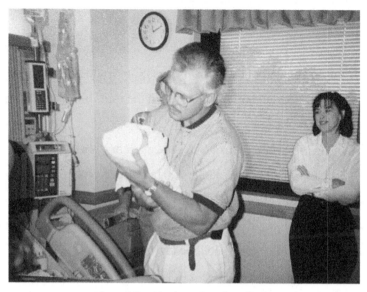

Me and Our Newborn Daughter Hailey

June 1999 Me and Hailey, 9 months' old

April, Layna and I

Me and My Babies Layna & Hailey

As life goes on the divorce between April and I was taking a toll on us all. I made some bad decisions after losing everything I owned to the court system and started drinking and drugging. I ended up at Dunklin Memorial Camp in Okeechobee, Florida for regeneration.

Please Come Home Daddy

A Poem by Dennis Blount
Inspired by The Holy Spirit

My children are very special,
the apple of my eye
The very best part of me,
for them I would die
When I do thing my way,
things get out of hand
When I stumble and fall,
just like a sinking sand

My children began to pray for me,
to the Father up above
Lord would you please help my Daddy,
he needs a little love
Lord, he didn't come home tonight
I forgive his sin and shame
He's the only Daddy I got,
and I still love him the same

Daddy please stop running, don't you even care?
Please come home tonight, Daddy it just aint fair
As I go to bed tonight, I cry myself to sleep
I wake up every hour just to take a peek

When I see your home I want to hold you tight
I think the Lord again,
I wont give up the fight
The Lord Hears my prayers,
victory is on the way
I know my daddy loves me,
because I heard him say

He will seek the Lord,
He will try to be
I saw him on his knees,
I heard him pray for me
I am proud of my daddy,
he has turned his life around
He gave his heart to Jesus,
and not he's heaven bound.

Praying together at Dunklin Memorial Camp - Hailey age 5, Layna age 11

Dunklin Memorial Camp – Visits with the Girls

The next few pages are worksheets and letters that my daughter Hailey
wrote. When my mother handed them to me I almost passed out. She
didn't say anything, but I knew she wasn't happy. I wanted to go to her
school in my defense but I knew that wasn't a good idea. I talked to
Hailey the best I knew how while inside I was dying of embarrassment. I
have kept them all these years and hope that by sharing them they will
keep another person from making my same mistakes. Children see and
know much more than we think.

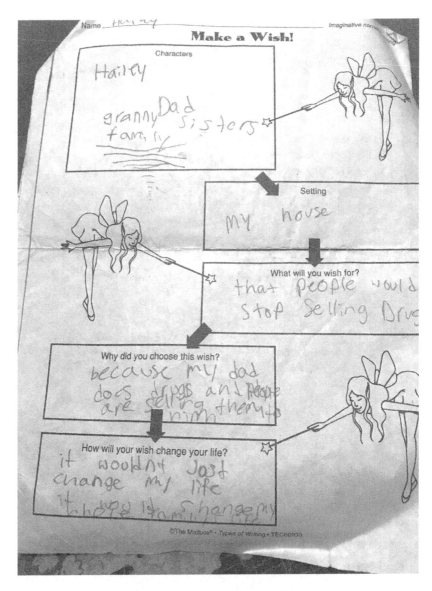

Name Hailey   Imaginative name

Make a Wish!

Characters

Hailey

granny Dad sisters
family

Setting

my house

What will you wish for?

that people would
stop selling Drug

Why did you choose this wish?

because my dad
does drugs and people
are selling them to
him

How will your wish change your life?

it wouldn't just
change my life
it would change my

©The Mailbox® • Types of Writing • TEC60930

A worksheet my Mom gave to me that my
daughter Hailey had worked on in school

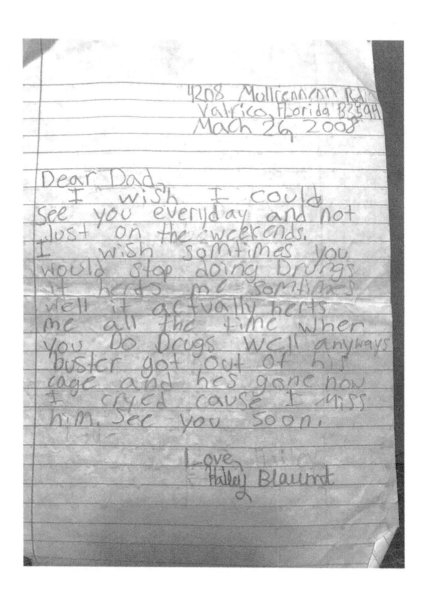

4208 Mullrennan Rd
Valrico, Florida 83594
Mach 26 2008

Dear Dad,
    I wish I could
see you everyday and not
just on the weekends.
I wish somtimes you
would stop doing Drugs
it herts me somtimes
well it actually herts
me all the time when
you Do Drugs well anyways
buster got out of his
cage and hes gone now
I cryed cause I miss
him. See you soon,

            Love,
            Halley Blount

My Wish

Hailey Bloom

You know why I wish people would stop selling Drugs because drugs are changing this world and changing peoples lifes and one of those lifes is my Dads my dad has been doing drugs sents hee was 15 and hes 50.

People sell drugs every where guess what person is buying them my dad if anybody in your family is doing drugs I know how you feel hert decaporded, not loved. And some times I feel like my dad doesnd love me anymore. and its hertful

Not Just people are selling drugs there makeseig drugs and there is millions of those peop who are in this world doing that. people are dying from it and its hard

and when you start you
can never stop.
Theres not just one type
of drug theres Millions
for entence weed my
dad smokes weed he
does all kinds of drugs
it herts my family my
sister and it expecueiy
herts my grnny wich
is my dads mom it
herts her sooo much
she has no life anymore.
And all those things
I just told you is why
I wish people would stop
selling/and making drugs.

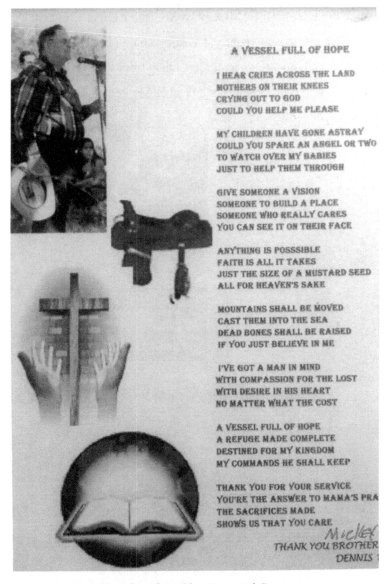

A VESSEL FULL OF HOPE

I HEAR CRIES ACROSS THE LAND
MOTHERS ON THEIR KNEES
CRYING OUT TO GOD
COULD YOU HELP ME PLEASE

MY CHILDREN HAVE GONE ASTRAY
COULD YOU SPARE AN ANGEL OR TWO
TO WATCH OVER MY BABIES
JUST TO HELP THEM THROUGH

GIVE SOMEONE A VISION
SOMEONE TO BUILD A PLACE
SOMEONE WHO REALLY CARES
YOU CAN SEE IT ON THEIR FACE

ANYTHING IS POSSSIBLE
FAITH IS ALL IT TAKES
JUST THE SIZE OF A MUSTARD SEED
ALL FOR HEAVEN'S SAKE

MOUNTAINS SHALL BE MOVED
CAST THEM INTO THE SEA
DEAD BONES SHALL BE RAISED
IF YOU JUST BELIEVE IN ME

I'VE GOT A MAN IN MIND
WITH COMPASSION FOR THE LOST
WITH DESIRE IN HIS HEART
NO MATTER WHAT THE COST

A VESSEL FULL OF HOPE
A REFUGE MADE COMPLETE
DESTINED FOR MY KINGDOM
MY COMMANDS HE SHALL KEEP

THANK YOU FOR YOUR SERVICE
YOU'RE THE ANSWER TO MAMA'S PRA
THE SACRIFICES MADE
SHOWS US THAT YOU CARE

Mickey

THANK YOU BROTHER
DENNIS

Founder of Dunklin Memorial Camp
Okachobee, FL

Founder brother, Mickey Evens, told me that God had given me a gift to write poetry. He said I should write a book. Not really knowing how to go about it, I knew from then on, I could and would one day. I knew when brother Mickey spoke, God was behind whatever he said.

Layna's First Barrel Race

Layna is ten years old now got a fever for barrel racing.
Her papa bought her first barrel horse Rose. She was a tough
mouth ole mare but could really spin them barrels. Every once in a
while she would get stubborn and turn the first barrel and then run
back to the gate. I would always tell Layna to turn around and
normally she would finish the pattern. One night at Turkey Creek
Stables speed show she done that. This time Layna came out of the
arena fighting mad and crying. I said, 'okay, let's go home'. She
said, 'I don't want to go home because there are more speed events
to come'. I told her, 'unless you change your attitude we are going
home'. She smiled a little bit and said okay. Also, I told her, 'until
you accept defeat with a good attitude you'll never become a
champion'. From then on her attitude stayed pretty good. She ran
the speed events a few years and was doing very well. She was
around 14 years old when she ran the fastest time in barrels and
won the high point trophy. I was very proud of her and her horse
Rose. I told her that night it's time for NBHA (National Barrel
Horse Association). With a big smile she said I'm ready for it. She
was glowing. She was one happy excited cowgirl. Her dream was
coming true.

Her second year running NBHA FL6 Layna qualified for
Youth World at Jackson Mississippi fair grounds. She was even
more excited because her Aunt Gay, Uncle Mark, and first cousins
lived in Magee, Mississippi and would be there to watch. She got
pretty upset that her horse BB didn't perform very well. I didn't

say anything to Layna but I knocked her horse out. Just kidding but felt like it. It was a good experience for Layna.

Turkey Creek Stable was the place Layna first started her barrel racing dream. Terry Barnes RIP and Peggy Womack were the owners of the stable. They always made sure the community kids had a horse to ride and learn on. Peggy still the owner and still taking care of the community kids.

One lady I would like to recognize is Judy McNab. She helped Layna get started with her dream. I learned a lot from her myself. She helped many kids get started with their barrel racing dream. Layna horse Rosa was in foal and when she got big as the moon we had to pull her off the barrels, breaking Layna's heart thinking she would have no barrel horse for a while. Judy McNab stepped up and loaned Layna her special horse Charlie. Judy kept my babies dream alive. I'll never forget it and I can't thank Judy enough.

I also want to recognize longtime friend Brenda Simmons. She has always and is still there for Layna. She has been a big part in Layna's barrel racing dream. She has helped me in many ways like she has done for many people. I can't thank her enough for all she's done for us.

Layna stopped barrel racing for a couple of years. Her and her sister, Hailey, started competition cheerleading. They both done very well and it was a good experience for them both.

In 2010 Layna became a senior at Durant High School and also worked at Panera Bread in Bloomingdale. At the time she was happy - driving to school and work and living the dream.

I was at work and received a phone call that changed my life forever. I was informed that Layna had had a stroke and a seizure. My heart broke and my faith in God expanded. Not understanding the situation and guilt set in quickly. I ask God to give me anything that would help me through the long road ahead. He instantly took me to John 9:1-7. In the presence of God, I was very relieved of the burden. My trust and faith in God grew to a much higher level. Hard for me to understand how a person gets through times like these without knowing God and my Lord and Savior Jesus Christ. My hope and prayer is that God will use this story to reach out to people that don't know him as their Lord and Savior. I have no idea what I would do without Him.

Layna was taken to Tampa General Hospital. After being there three months with many MRI's, CAT Scans, EEG's, and other tests it was still not determined what caused Layna to stoke and seizure. Layna would scream and cry, begging me to not let them take her for another MRI or test. There was nothing I could do but turn my head and look to God. It was killing me. I was dying inside. God spoke to me at one of those moments saying, 'now you see how hard it was for me to turn my back on my son Jesus when he was hanging and dying on the cross for you'. Throughout this journey God was always working behind the scenes and smoothing things out.

Layna was taking so much medication to control the seizures. She got better and was sent home. About a month went by and Layna had a stroke and seizure again. This time it was worse. She went back to Tampa General Hospital.

Layna's mother, April, for the first two months never left the hospital. There is nothing else like the love of a mother. I worked six days a week, then to the hospital and on home to take care of horses. I would stay overnight with Layna on Saturdays. Hailey was 12 years old and in good hands with her stepdad, John Monjure.

I called Hailey every day and would see her on weekends. She seemed and said she was doing ok with her sister being sick. To our surprise she was struggling. Hailey had her struggles with her sister being sick but as always she preserved through them with Gods help. Very often Hailey puts on her big sister shoes.

At this point Layna was getting worse. The doctors didn't have answers for why Layna was sick. All we could do was trust God for another miracle of healing in Layna's life. It was life threating. Death once again was knocking at Layna's life door at the point of Layna wanting to give up. We all had to encourage her to keep fighting. She would always cowgirl up and keep going with the help of her Savior. She now was down to 70lbs. and could not eat. They placed a feed tube through her nose. She did not like that at all. She kept on pulling the tube out. To prevent her from pulling it out they placed mittens on her hands.

Funny time was when her grandmother Sharon staying overnight. Layna convinced her that if she would take the mittens off she promised not to pull the tube out. With the love of a grandmother she agreed. It wasn't long before the tube was out again. It was extremely hard for us all but Layna's deceiving sweet talk didn't work for her again.

Layna had the Spirit of God all over her because she kept a pretty good attitude most all of the time. Even though she also went blind and couldn't walk. Her Goliath was huge but her faith and trust in God was greater. I kept encouraging her by saying that God was not going to let his already miracle child die. That just didn't make any sense to me at all. I always kept in mind what God gave me in the beginning John 9:1-7. It's all for His glory. It gave some peace. I was ok with that even though it was still extremely hard to watch. By this time we were getting extremely desperate for a doctor that would know what was wrong with Layna.

Layna's doctor, Dr. Dekker, said he thought he knew what was wrong with Layna. He said he knew of a doctor (Dr. John Shoffner) that studied mitochondrial disease and was located at Scottish Rite Children's Hospital in Atlanta, Georgia. We were told that he was one of only two doctors in America that studied mitochondrial disorder. It's more common today. With hope in our hearts Layna and her mom boarded a med jet and headed north to Atlanta. It was a blessing that my sister Brenda and her family lived in Atlanta. It made things somewhat more convenient for our family to go stay a few days.

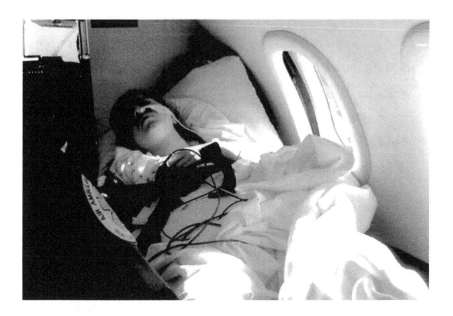

Med Jet to Scottish Rite, Atlanta, GA

Dr. John Shoffner at Scottish Rite Children's Hospital determined that Layna had Mitochondrial Disease a blood cell disorder. She was lacking the cell that produces energy to her brain in return caused brain damage. Now what do we do? We continued to pray and trust God. The previous doctors had Layna taking 78 pills a day. The doctor at Scottish Rite Children's Hospital weaned her down to about 40 some pills a day. Still today she takes 26 pills a day to help prevent stroke and seizure and to build the blood cell up that she is lacking.

Christmas was just a few days away. It was time for me to go and see my baby. My work place JVS contracting has been in many ways a blessing to my family. Through JVS my children and I are covered with health care insurance with United Health Care. Thank you John Simon, owner of JVS, for covering the airfare to fly me out to Atlanta

*Mitochondrial diseases are a group of disorders caused by dysfunctional **mitochondria**, the **organelles** that generate energy for the cell. Mitochondria are found in every cell of the human body except **red blood cells**, and convert the energy of food molecules into the **ATP** that powers most cell functions.*

*Mitochondrial diseases are sometimes (about 15% of the time) caused by mutations in the **mitochondrial DNA** that affect mitochondrial function. Other mitochondrial diseases are caused by **mutations** in **genes** of the **nuclear DNA**, whose gene products are imported into the mitochondria as well as acquired mitochondrial conditions. Mitochondrial diseases take on unique characteristics both because of the way the diseases are often inherited and because mitochondria are so critical to cell function. The subclass of these diseases that have neuromuscular disease symptoms are often called a **mitochondrial myopathy**.*

to be with my baby during Christmas time. It snowed in Atlanta on Christmas day. I heard someone say, the last time it snowed on Christmas day in Atlanta was I think 1848. It was a special time to be in Atlanta.

Scottish Rite Children's Hospital is truly an amazing hospital. It has a chapel for church and prayer. I could actually sense the presence of the Holy Spirit of God when I first entered the building. My first thought was I serve an awesome God. When I thought there was not a way, all the time He was making a way. Layna's grandmother's pastor's dad, Evangelist John Todd, gave her a scripture to stand on: *Psalm 118:17 Instead of dying I will live and proclaim what the Lord has done.* That scripture has certainly stuck with her ever since.

I WILL NOT DIE, BUT LIVE, AND I WILL PROCLAIM WHAT THE LORD HAS DONE. -- PSALM 118:17

Layna getting a visit from friend Brittie Crum.

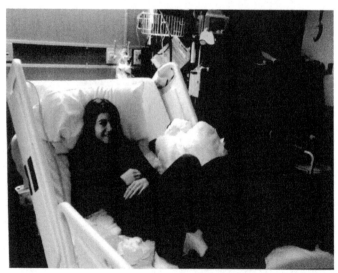

Layna in her room smiling although she couldn't see a thing.

There were times Layna would panic and say the room is filling up with water. I would just tell her no baby that's the Holy Spirit. It just looks like water. That would somewhat calm her down. It was extremely hard to watch the effects of the pain meds. It was time for therapy and rehab. I watched Layna struggle putting two and two together and even colors. Speech was also hard for her. Working with other patients and hospital staff Layna started making progress. I was there the second week of her stay. At the end of that week Layna's vision was trying to get better. She would say I can see a little bit. She started eating better and gaining strength and weight. Prayers once again reaching the Throne Room of God. The wine maker was in her room. Before I left for home and back to work I witnessed Layna with a walker take her first few steps back to the saddle.

With her faith in God she would many times say, I can't wait to get back home to ride Rose. I said to her, keep fighting and God will make that happen for you. She was at the Scottish Rite Children's Hospital about a month longer before returning home.

Still in a wheelchair, I witnessed her going to a walker to a cane and then on her own. With her strong cowgirl will and Gods help she just kept going forward. About six months went by and Layna had been begging the doctor and her mother to release her to ride her horse Rose. This is where I got very emotional. Layna would say I'm fine I can ride. It didn't come too soon for me either. I understood the love and passion for riding horses.

The day finally came. The doctor released Layna to ride her horse and her mother also released her as long as she wore a helmet while running barrels. Against her tough cowgirl pride she agreed to wear the helmet. June 2011 I'll never forget the moment. I was shouting glory be to God and crying like a baby when I saw Layna ride her horse Rose through that pasture gate. It was truly amazing what God had done for Layna.

She had the biggest smile I had ever seen. I'm talking ear to ear. I was one happy daddy. God done put my baby back in the saddle. It was cowgirl up. I'm telling ya'll there was therapy going on at the barn. The wine Maker done showed up again with his new wine. There was a healing going on in Durant. Layna literally looked death in the eye and said my God is bigger. INSTEAD.

She's a Running Miracle
A Poem by Dennis Blount

Her eye sight isn't 100%
Focus on the barrel halfway in between
But she keeps on running
Making sure to accomplish her dream

No peripheral vision to the left
No feeling in her feet
But she keeps on running
And she's hard to beat

I push her real hard
She gets mad when I do
Nothing but a fighter
And a sweetheart too

She's got a handicap sticker
This is true
But when she turns and burns
She just might fool you

She's my oldest daughter
I'm proud to say
She just keeps on running
I thank God she's here to stay

I just can't do it
I've never heard her say
Trusting in her Savior.
"God help me" she would pray

God's amazing love
She's an inspiration to us all
She's a running miracle
On her horse strong and tall

You can find Layna and her horse Rose on the front cover of *In the Field Magazine* Plant City, FL April 15-May 15, 2011 page 54 is the story my cousin Howard Blount wrote.

Each day with the touch of Gods hand and a multitude of prayers, Layna became stronger. She had to deal daily with headaches, bladder pain, and leg muscle pain and still does today. With her strong cowgirl will, determination, and passion for barrel racing she eventually got back to it.

Layna would say she couldn't feel her feet in the stirrups and couldn't see the next barrel until she got about half way to it. With faith in God, the horse and Layna's natural ability to ride I told her not to worry the horse can see the barrels just hang on tight and ride like you know how.

Funny one time she ran the pattern and her boot was hanging by itself in the stirrup. The whole time her foot would be hanging out. Sometimes her boot would fall off. She would just laugh, cowgirl up and keep going. I've come to realize that when a cowgirl gets the desire to become a champion barrel racer there's no obstacle going to stop them. Barrel racing is difficult. It's not easy running high speed with precision stops and turns. You have to be born with the God giving passion and ability to do it.

Hailey's Graduation Photo Taken by Photographer Stephanie Humphries
Wearing Granny's (My Mother Mary) Dress

Layna and Hailey

To encourage Layna, I started barrel racing at the age of 54. I found out really quick just how difficult it was. For about a year or so I would say I'm too old and can't do this. But with passion to race horses and being competitive and a desire to keep Layna encouraged I stayed with it. Today I'm glad I didn't throw in the towel because Layna and I have a blast competing at the barrel races.

©2017 Don Bonnice

©2017 Don Bonnice

Layna's mother had told me that God had spoken to her heart saying Layna would walk the stage with her 2010 graduating class. I believed God with her. There was a school teacher working at Tampa General Hospital during Layna's stay there. Gary worked Layna through passing grades and she passed FCAT. Sure enough Layna walked the stage and received her diploma with her 2010 Durant High School graduating class. Through tears it was a sight to see. God is good and faithful to His Word.

Layna was making progress running barrels on her old horse Rose. Barrel Racing at Turkey Creek Stables speed events where she first got started. She was getting all she could out of Rose at 25 years old. Layna needed a new barrel horse. I had a gelding out of Rose name Mr Blount. I had started him on the race track and he was doing pretty good through his training. We put him in the barrel pen and it didn't take him long to catch on to the pattern.

Layna joined back with NBHAFL6 and started doing good on Mr. Blount. One thing I have learned in all this, it's not over until God says it's over. Even though at times it looked impossible with God's help Layna is living her dream.

Once again, *In the Field Magazine* came to our farm for a follow up on Layna's progress (Issue July 15-August 15, 2014 story page 53).

Photo by Photographer Tanya Kozlovsky

Cowgirl Up

A Poem by Dennis Blount

The odds have been against her
Since the day she was born
Five percent chance of living
My heart was torn

I looked up to Heaven
Down on my knees
Asking God for a miracle
"Will you save her please?"

Doctors had their doubts
My faith was strong
Speaking God's Word
Over my blood, flesh and bone

My daughter lived through it
As she saddled up her horse
She Cowgirled Up
On a barrel horse of course

NBHA Finals
Made it all the way
Guts heart and passion
Tough price to pay

Wasn't over yet
Hard times just ahead
"18 years late..."
Layna Blount said INSTEAD

A disease took control
Death knocking at her door again
And with a fearless heart
She said to Jesus her Savior her friend

"Instead of dying, I shall live
Proclaim what the Lord has done!"
She's got nerves of steel
Whenever she's under the gun

Four years later
In the Master's Hand
2014 NBHA FL State Championships
On God's Word she does stand

She rides like the wind
As she drinks the Communion cup
Trusting in her Savior
Cowgirl Up

2014 NBHA Florida Championships Kissimmee. Layna Blount on Mr. Blount INSTEAD made two good go rounds and qualified for finals. She placed 4D 8th is finals. Nearly 900 entries God was really blessing my baby girl and her confidence was boiling over. I was on cloud nine. Hailey on Maggie made a couple of good runs in the youth but fail in the cracks. She rides very well.

Funny time was when we got to the state show I parked by our stalls to unload. I didn't know it was a fire lane area no signs. We went ahead and rode for about an hour and were cooling off our horses. Here comes this excited lady loudly demanding I move my truck right this second like there was a fire. I told her soon as my horse cooled I would move it. She got louder and threatened to disqualify us all. That's when my scooter Hailey got right in her face and told her over my dead body you will disqualify my sister. Hailey doesn't hesitate putting on big sister britches and defend her older sister Layna.

Layna on TL Hollywood SMARTZ (Faith)

Layna running barrels 2015 NBHAFL6 was very productive. She started out running two horses Mr. Blount and TL Hollywood SMARTZ (Faith). Thanks to Brooke Bluhm for working with Layna to buy Faith. Layna's dream horse and she has certainly taken good care of Layna. I think Layna's best run on Faith was at Smokehouse Arena. 120 entries she placed 1d5th. When things like this happen it really gives Layna a boost and keeps her going forward.

Faith can run full speed to the first barrel stop and turn but Layna is not able to. One show at Double R Arena she came flying in to the first barrel and I thought oh no. Sure enough Faith stopped to turn Layna hit the ground hard. Once again she cowgirled up and move on.

A while back we were at a night show it was raining on and off. The arena was muddy and had some water puddles. The barrels were caked with mud. There was a lot of glare with the bright white lights Layna up on Faith came back to the gate to tell me she could not see the first barrel. I calmly told her once again with faith in God and her horse that her horse would take her to the barrel and if she could not see it by then pull her up. INSTEAD turned around took off and win 2d that night. Praise the Lord again.

Layna is allowed to work part time at Panera Bread in Bloomingdale as she feels like it. Thank you Panera Bread. It's a big blessing for Layna and her family.

A recent barrel race Layna win 2nd finishing 13th out of 176 entries. It's a miracle every time she runs. It's truly amazing what God is doing in Layna's life.

At the 2015 Florida State Championship show Layna Realized she couldn't muster up enough energy to run two horsed any longer. Running on through 2015 with her horse Faith she done very well. She qualified for World Championships show in Perry, Georgia. With her disability at 24 years old she's going strong. She keeps a good attitude even though she can't drive herself anywhere. I commend and thank her all the time for not complaining about her condition.

In the past four years, Layna has had lite seizure four to five times and went to Tampa General for observation. She would stay three to four days. God got her through it and she moved on.

Still today her balance, vision, and feeling in her feet are not 100% but to watch her go it's hard to see her disabilities. She has driven a car but with the limited feeling in her feet it's scary for her. She will load her bull dog Lila up on the golf cart and drive around the pasture and up and down Blount Road. She can also saddle her horse to trail ride or work barrels. She just keeps on living life. Praise the Lord.

A while back Layna ran barrels at night. The arena lights were bright white and she had no problem seeing the barrels. I told her it's dark out the gate and when you're coming home from the 3rd barrel you may have trouble seeing where the gate is. Sure enough she couldn't see the gate. Heading to the fence she bobbled a little bit but hung on and was ok. Cowgirl up and once again God taking care of my baby.

Recently, we ran again at night where the arena lights were soft lite yellow and I was hoping she would be able to see. She went in turned first and second barrel fine. All of a sudden she pulled up and took off back to first and second barrel. She pulled up again saying I can't see. As Layna continues to travel down this barrel racing trail she may encounter more obstacles. We always have and will trust God to get her through them all.

My hat is off to NBHA directors and all those that participate and give their time coordinating barrel races for any reason. You all are a blessing to many people. Dreams are fulfilled because of you all giving your time. Thank you and God bless each and every one of you. Let's don't forget the tractor drivers. Thank you all.

My heart and desire for writing and sharing this true story is that it will reach people and families with similar trails in their life. I'm hoping it will give you hope and inspiration. If you do not know Jesus Christ as your Lord and Savior, here are a few scriptures for you to read out loud and find Him, right now, as your Lord and Savior and receive your salvation. Remember, Matthew 19:26 With God All Things Are Possible.

11 They triumphed over him
by the blood of the Lamb
and by the word of their testimony;
they did not love their lives so much
as to shrink from death.

Revelation 12:11 (NIV)

SCRIPTURES

*9 I am the gate; whoever enters through me will be
saved.[a] They will come in and go out, and find
pasture. 10 The thief comes only to steal and kill and destroy;
I have come that they may have life, and have it to the full.*

John 10:9-10 (NIV)

*16 For God so loved the world that he gave His one and only
Son, that whoever believes in him shall not perish but have
eternal life.*

John 3:16 (NIV)

*9 If you declare with your mouth, "Jesus is Lord," and
believe in your heart that God raised him from the dead, you
will be saved. 10 For it is with your heart that you believe
and are justified, and it is with your mouth that you profess
your faith and are saved.*

Romans 10:9-10 (NIV)

*Now grow in the Lord Jesus Christ:
18 But grow in the grace and knowledge of our Lord and
Savior Jesus Christ. To him be glory both now and forever!
Amen.*

2 Peter 3:18 (NIV)

Made in United States
Orlando, FL
08 May 2022

17651990R00049